Vera's Lot

By

Vera M. Goupillot

Lachmannstrasse Berlin

Vera Margot Kuhnke, first born to Wilhelm Hermann Kuhnke and Johanna (Hannah) Elfriede Kuhnke (nee Kaschke) on the 20 December 1941 at Number 2 Lachmannstrasse near the centre of Berlin, in Germany.

Me and my mum Hannah
1941

My father Wilhelm is recorded on my birth certificate as being a feuerwehrmann (fireman) in the Berlin Fire Brigade. We believe that this was a wartime appointment as a fire-fighter. This had to be one of the most difficult tasks for any fire fighter, the blitzing of Berlin continued to get worse as the war progressed, culminating in the street fighting and shelling by the Russians in 1945. The wartime fire-fighter's uniform was not unlike that of a soldier and a number of firemen were shot in the heat of battle before being properly identified.

My Dad in the Berlin Fire Brigade
1943

The only thing I remember about living in Lachmmanstrasse was biting a lump out of cousin Manfreds arm because he wouldn't let me pass him on the stairs. He was quick to show me the scar in 1971 when we met up again. We also showed each other scars on our heads from injuries received trying to get conkers down from the trees in the square at the front of our house.

Return to Lachmannstrasse with Mum & Aunty Trutchen
1992

Mum said that we had a pet chimpanzee; unfortunately it had to go because it became jealous when I was born. She would maybe have had less trouble if she had got rid of me and kept the chimp!!

The family was in show business when I came on the scene. Dad was a top class acrobat until he was badly hurt in a fall from the highwire, he then resorted to juggling and conjuring with mam as his assistant. They played under the stage name of Cunelli, and were considered to be one of the top acts in the country. They received the top pay within the profession; remember this was before television.

They played all the big variety shows around the country and with all the big circuses of the time like Circus Henny, Circus Robert Danials, and the Erich Fischer Circus.
When I was two years old we became the 2 ½ Cunellis with klein (little) Vera doing various tricks including balancing on the top of a ladder perched on fathers chin. I was in trouble one day for stopping the performance to pickup chocolates and sweets that had been thrown on the stage.

Me probably three or four, the half of the 2 ½ Conellis

Whilst performing for the Russians after the fall of Berlin, I was on top of the ladder, which was balanced on dad's chin, when the lights suddenly went out, I fell from the ladder right into the open top of the piano, when light was restored I was dragged from the piano bleeding and in pain and told to smile and carry on with the performance, the show must go on, blood tears and all!!

Dad and I showing off!!

On another occasion Mum and the group, dancers and the various other performers, were getting on the company coach after a show in Kiev when a Russian soldier tried to stop them. She bundled them all onto the coach and set off hell for leather with the Russian taking pot shots at the back of the bus, I remember that some of the costumes at the back had bullet holes, but thankfully no one was hurt. Being well known entertainers we were expected to perform for the forces and my mum remembers that the Russians paid up for a show without hesitation but it was hard work sometimes getting the money from the

Americans and the French, even harder getting it from the Brits, they quite often didn't pay at all.

Berlin was bombed day and night and towards the end, shelled with long and then short range artillery. This meant that the people had to remain in the air raid shelters. Our shelter was part of the Zoo flak tower (for anti-aircraft guns) that the gunners were meant to live in but at that time they were in almost constant action and usually had to sleep at their guns. These towers were virtually bomb proof but they still shook when a bomb landed close by, the noise was deafening and towards the end it seemed to be almost continuous day and night.

Food was scarce and could usually only be bought on the black-market at ridiculous prices. Most people including my mum could not get any food at all at one time. Water had to be collected from outside and it was during one of these dashes out that my two baby brothers were killed by shrapnel whilst in the pram, she didn't know they had been hit until she returned to the shelter.

The situation became even more desperate with some people starving to death. During one such period our shelter was visited by the infamous Herman Goring, he was so distressed by what he saw that he ordered his henchmen to bring food and water to the shelter for the sick children. Mum believes that without this intervention we may well have died.

During a lull in the fighting mum set off with me in a pushchair to Grandma's house on the outskirts of Berlin about twenty miles away and past areas where heavy fighting with the Russians was still going on. She recalled looking around a corner, and seeing tanks in the street, she ran off just as a heavy explosion blew the corner away completely.

When we arrived after what must have been a horrendous journey, Mum was blind and in a complete state of collapse. Grandad had to push her three miles to the doctors in a wheelbarrow.

Life goes on in Berlin but not for everyone!
1945

The only things I can remember of our stay there is gazing at a painting of a little girl in the rain with an umbrella in the bedroom of Grandmas house, and sitting on the edge of a stream eating cherries with Auntie Gretchen. I can't remember school at that time but I do remember my private music teacher tapping her cane on the floor to keep me in step, she would make me do the splits between two stools, I was terrified of that but even more scared of her, she was a real tarter.

We suffered again in 1948 when the Russians sealed the city from the west and starvation was again a factor in our lives. The only route open for food, fuel and other supplies was by air. The British and American air forces did a fantastic job of keeping us going until the Russians realised that with the help of the allies we would not be beaten.

8 This Avro York took part in the Berlin Airlift
Derived from the Lancaster that did so much damage to us in 1945 now returns to help keep us alive with 29,000 flights. A total of over 5000 tons per day by all services.

Dad would sometimes beat my Mam, I suppose it was his highly strung artistic temperament, I recall visiting her in hospital, children were not allowed inside so she used to chat to me out of the window and throw bits of food down to me. It was as a result of these beatings that the doctor advised mother to leave him for a while, which she did, Dad always came after her and said he wouldn't hurt her again but he always did. In the end it was decided that her and I would leave the country and go abroad for a while.

From Germany to the England

There was a scheme in operation at that time that would allow German women to go to the USA, Australia, Canada or the UK as aliens (they would be called au-pairs now), the idea was that they would live with a family for a year for just their keep, this was to allow the receiving family to recoup the travelling expenses. Mum would have preferred the USA because she had a relative over there, however, a place in England came up first she had to take it or risk going back to the bottom of the list. Mum was allowed to bring me, I remember saying goodbye to dad at the airport, lots of tears from us all but it was too late to change our minds.

They gave us fruit on the aircraft and I didn't like the orange very much, nobody told me that the skin had to come off! The airhostess was very nice and taught me to say please and thank you in English.

When we arrived in the UK we were ushered into a large hangar stripped off and dusted down with some kind of de-lousing powder, mum was furious, I was just freezing cold. They put us in a hotel for the night where I got fleas, English fleas!!

We were taken by train and taxi to Stokesley to live with a Mr. and Mrs. Gee at The Close, built in 1733, since renamed *The Old Rectory*, a large house just out of town. We had our own rooms and I think we were reasonably happy there, well most of the time - it was understandably difficult for any Germans coming to England so soon after the War.

The Old Rectory, Stokesley, our first home in the UK

The kids at school taught me some English on the first day, and when I returned home Mrs. Gee asked what I had learned, so I told her, "Vera is a little bugger." She was so shocked that she whacked me around the ear, mother went berserk and told her never to raise her hand to me again, Mum could, and did very often, but nobody else could. Mum gave me another clip when she found out what I had said. That nearly cost us a trip back to Germany. I was then sent to a language school in Redcar to learn English properly, even that didn't stop the kids beating me up, until they found out that I could fight back hard when I had to.

Mum was divorced in that first year and it was decided by the authorities that we could stay on in England (still as aliens) provided we reported to the Police every year or if ever we moved house or planned to leave the county for any reason. It was not until 1962 that the authorities took us off the alien list. All this meant was that we didn't have to report our movements around the UK to the Police, we still needed our German passports.

A colleague of Mr Gee, Tony Ayton, a wealthy businessman, befriended mother and it was from this relationship that Shirley, Monica, and Tony came into the world. Tony was quite well off and treated us all to the good life. When the year was up, and Mum finished working for the Gee's he moved us into Holbrook House in Great Ayton. Mother and Tony had planned to marry but unfortunately Tony became very ill and he tried to get mum to marry him in the hospital, She said that she would when he recovered, however that was not to be and he died suddenly. His family rejected any claim that Mum may have had to his estate. She was left penniless with four children to bring up and had to move out of Holbrook House into a series of small flats in Ayton. Because I was so much older than the other kids in the family I had to live in digs.

Tony Ayton with me, Mum, a friend holding baby Shirley and Susie Bennison

It was not all doom and gloom, we kids had some great times. We would take a bottle of water and some jam butties and ramble over the moors or walk to Stokesley with the little kids in the prams, go to the pictures or just play in the park or climb Roseberry Topping.

I was shopped by someone for losing control of the pram with our Shirley in, I was taking the pram down the Chapel Steps when the pram decided that it could go down better on it's own, I watched in horror as it rolled over and over hitting most of the steps and then landing upside down at the bottom, Shirley was completely unhurt, but my backside was sore for days.

I was in trouble again for nicking off school for a day, when I got home Mum asked what we had been learning that day, I told her a very convincing story that my mate and I had contrived. She listened carefully then gave me a good thrashing. What I didn't know was that the school had been closed down for the day for some reason that I wasn't aware of. That could only happen to me.

One night I was returning from the dance at Stokesley and I was sitting resting on a bench in the dark when a cow suddenly poked it's head over the fence right next to me, I don't know who ran the fastest when I screamed, me or the cow!

I left school at 15 and started work at the Richpack Egg Packing Station and lived with Robinet and John Runack, she treated me rough and expected me to come home from work and do all the cleaning cooking and looking after the kids. She locked me out one night because she had her boyfriend staying while her husband was on nights. I slept on the doorstep. When I went to work the next morning and the manager wanted to know why I was in such a state, he reported this to the authorities and I was moved in with Mr. and Mrs. Cook, they were very nice to me but I had to move again when their son returned home to live.

I then went to live with Auntie Susie Bennison, Mum had met Susie, a German girl, just after arriving in England. Harry, her husband, had met Susie whilst serving with the Army in Germany and they have remained friends ever since, I was very happy living with them.

54 Linden Grove Great Ayton where I lived with the Bennison family

As I have said, I worked at the Egg Packing Station when I left school and spent most of the time collecting eggs in a van from farms all over the North Riding (North Yorkshire as it is now). Most of the people we met treated us well and I enjoyed the travelling, that is until the van tipped over as we climbed the snow covered bank near the Jolly Sailors Inn on the Yorkshire moors, the driver, Bill Bains his little dog, Mitsy, and I were okay but I can still see the scrambled eggs flowing down the road.

During this period I made friends with Jean Goupillot, at the time she was working at the Friends School in Great Ayton. She got engaged to Albert and I was invited to an engagement party at her house in Middlesborough. It was there that I first met John; he was waiting for us at the United Bus Station in Middlesborough. We were introduced and almost the first thing he said was that he was going to marry me - blooming cheek, mind he did look nice in his flashy Scots Greys Army uniform. When he came on leave he would wait for me outside the factory and all the girls would peep out to see what he looked like and say how lucky I was, I used to say that he was the lucky one!

We courted for a year but because he was stationed in South Wales he couldn't get home very often. He was domobed in December 1957 and joined Middlesborough Fire Brigade, He had to go to the Fire Training School at Felling near Gateshead for twelve weeks. He finished on the Friday and we got married on Saturday the 8 March 1958.

8th March 1958 with John's Dad, Sister Jean his Mum and Lily Jones a friend

Marriage and Beyond

We were married at the Registry Office on College Road in the Boro and spent our first night at John's mums, the following day we moved into a two-roomed flat at 17 Orwell Street in the centre of town. We had to move the little bits of furniture that we had acquired on a handcart, as the snow got deeper the job became more and more difficult, but we managed. That evening we found a one-shilling piece (6 new pence) on the pavement outside of the house that gave us enough to go to the pictures. I remember that John put on his demob suit trousers, army socks and shoes and his Fire Brigade jacket to look something like a blazer and flannels. At least it was warmer at the pictures than in the flat; we couldn't have the fire on because we had no money for coal and in any event we couldn't get any until the Monday.

John started work at the Fire Station on the Monday and I started as the chief cashier at Newhouses Emporium in Middlesborough. I worked in a glass cage in the basement and the cash was sent to me in brass cylinders that were sent around by compressed air along tubes from all the different departments. It was quite a responsible job for a sixteen year old, but it was great fun handling all the cash!

Newhouses Corner where I worked as cashier at sixteen years old.

The landlord at Orwell Street, Stan, was a Postman, he had left for work after me one morning and John was in bed after a night shift. We had a gas ring for heating the water and Stan had left an aluminium pan boiling on the ring, after a while the water evaporated and the pan melted over the ring sending the flames into the curtains and down onto the wooden table, fortunately John was awakened by the sound of crashing from downstairs. When he went to investigate he found the kitchen blazing, he ran up and down stairs with buckets of water and swears that that was the hardest fire he had fought either before or since. He had just started work at the Fire Station and no way was he going to call his mates to help, he would never have lived it down.

Stan was divorced from his wife and after a while she found out that he was renting the flat so we had to move. We moved in with John's Mum and Dad, at 12 Thirlby Close Berwick Hills Estate. In those early days mum didn't really take to me and there was some friction at times. I wasn't good enough for her little Johnny!!

We used to go to the dances at the old Hippodrome, I would wear a loose skirt with layers of stiffened petticoats underneath and John would try to dress like a Teddy-boy and his hair was curled and fashioned into a Tony Curtis style. We had live bands at the dances in those days and if someone took centre stage the spot-lights would go onto them and the band would pick up the mood, John, the big show-off, would sometimes get into the limelight with my work-mate Yvonne Golding, at one time he was throwing me over his shoulder and pulling me under his legs, I have never felt so embarrassed in all my life. It didn't matter whether it was a Bop, the Twist, Jive or Jitter-bug or any other dance, he would always dance them to Charleston steps, he still does, I haven't the heart to ask him to learn new steps.

I had a bad time whilst I was pregnant with Michael, I discovered a cyst on my spine, the hospital staff gave me a local anaesthetic, these weren't very good in those days and I could feel them hacking away at me. I had to go straight home on the bus, no ambulance or taxis for the working classes, I felt such a wally standing on an almost empty bus, I could hardly walk and felt very faint all the way home. John had to change the dressings every day for weeks because it would not heal up. I eventually had to return to hospital for them to drain the wound, remove part of the base of my spine and sew it up again.

Our Michael was expected to be born at home but complications set in and I was rushed to the maternity hospital. John was called from work and was told that there was no hope for the baby but that I may be alright. Michael must have sensed that the knife was going to be used so he stopped being awkward and was born naturally and without any further fuss. If that wasn't bad enough John came to visit me wearing special glasses because he had his eyes burned at a fire that morning.

Michael with Aunty Evelyn at 12 Thirlby Close Berwick Hills Estate M'bro

John had a big fire at Marton Hall in Stewart's Park, it lasted quite a few days so I took Michael in the pushchair and we had pop and sandwiches with John and his crew on the big lawn at the back. The fire was still burning when they got back to work so they hadn't missed anything!!

1960 John and Billy Lee at the top of the ladder at the Marton Hall fire

We bought our first car in 1959, a 1931 Morris 7. When these cars were new you could have them in any colour you wanted provided it was black. It cost me a fortune in black boot polish and brasso. It was so old fashioned; even then, that I felt embarrassed riding around in it. John thought it was great; he would take us to the seaside, drop us off, then stay in the car leaning out of the window posing with his sunglasses on. I was even more embarrassed when he and Billy Lee set off on their part time job, window cleaning, with the ladders sticking out of the sunroof, it looked like something out of a Laurel and Hardy film. Worse was yet to come, John's dad very reluctantly agreed to come with us on a trip to Eston Hills, on the way back the heavens opened, we had to stop until it cleared because the windscreen wipers were hopeless. When we set off again we hadn't gone far when we hit a big puddle in the road, a column of water shot up a hole where the handbrake came through and cascaded over father half drowning him. He roared at John to stop the car, got out, and he set off to walk dripping wet, nothing we could do would persuade him to get back into that car, or any other of our cars for that matter, for years. Even our, much posher, or so John would have me believe, 1936 Morris 8 would not tempt him.

The 1936 Morris 8 very posh compared to the 1931 Morris 7

We moved in with John's Aunt Evelyn in Union Street. She had broken her leg falling down the stairs, and it was easier to live there than travelling up and down from Berwick Hills Estate. We piled the furniture on top of the little car, it had no roof rack, I panicked when a Policeman stopped us outside of the

Town Hall because of the size of the load, he and John started chatting about the Cannon Street riots they had both been to the night before, we then drove off. I think he had forgotten why he had stopped us in the first place. I then got a good job as the manageress; there was no one to manage, as there was only the boss and I, at Denega's Fruit Shop on Corporation Road until we moved into the caravan at Stokesley.

The Saga of the Caravans

Our first caravan was an old banger that we had while waiting for our new one to be built and delivered. At least we were on our own at last, even if it was in the middle of a cow field at Mill Riggs Farm Stokesley, owned by Frank and Mary Kennedy. Mum also got a caravan and moved with us. The life was hard, we had to collect water from the farm and bury the toilet waste from the Elson chemical toilets. The field was a quagmire in the bad weather and we had to leave wellington boots in a box near the gate.

It was here that we first met Helen and Peter Dawson, they had a caravan in the same field. As I have said, it was a hard life but we did have some great times. We had to entertain ourselves, we played practical jokes on each other, one night we were going to bed to find that our night clothes had been sewn up at the neck and arms. Helen and Peter didn't know that we had removed the mattress from their pull-down bed until bedtime, they had to get dressed again to come looking for it.

Someone knocked on the door of our van and John stepped out of the door straight into a basin of water that mother had planted. She often tried to creep up to our van in the dark to get up to some mischief, she could sometimes be seen in the moonlight, so, one night she set off right around the field keeping close to the hedge, rather than come directly over the open field, just as she was about to knock on the door, John, who had watched her go all the way around, shone the torch onto her face under the van, she nearly died with fright.

The worst one they played was on me, I came home from work one night to find that the pigs had got into the box of groceries that we had had delivered. The food was scattered all over, bits of bread, corn flakes, battered and bent tins. I was heart broken, we had no money to replace them, I could have killed them when I found out that it was all a wind-up, they had opened the fence a bit, taken the labels of the tins and scattered scrap bits of food around near the door and out into the field. But I had the last laugh; they hadn't marked the tins, so I served them up as they came, beans and apricots, Irish stew and pilchards, tomatoes and peas!! They didn't try that one again.

John was teaching me to ride the motorbike in the field, he told me what to do then held on to the back as we set off across the field.
"Close the throttle," he shouted.
"What's a throttle?"
"The one on the right," he roared.
"Oh that one!"
He didn't tell me which way to turn it, yep, I turned it the wrong way and off we went belting over the rough ground with John's feet barely touching the ground, and me leaping into the air each time we hit a bump, I was terrified, the others watching thought it was great and wanted us to do it again after they got the camera out, no chance, my place is on the back

seat. Well, most of the time, John came to pick me up from work one day and drove off before I had chance to sit down properly, I felt such a twit standing legs apart at the side of the busy road, at least in the old Morris 7 no one could see the embarrassment on my face!!

Mike and I with the James motorbike

Once we got settled in Mum looked after the kids and I went back to work, this time at the Beacon Garage petrol station at Marton Bungalow. It was owned by George Hardwick the Middlesborough and England football player, and it gave me the chance to meet lots of celebrities that came to visit, Pat Phoenix (Else Tanner), Tommy Steel, Bobby Charlton, Bobby Moore, Brian Clough and many others.

The new caravan arrived the Bluebird Defiant 28 feet long 8 ½ feet wide, separate bedroom, bathroom, toilet, kitchen and a really nice lounge, our dream home, except that it was still in the mud. It cost us £600 on tick, that was a lot of money in those days.

John was earning only £9 a week from the Fire Brigade and what ever he could make part time, my wages kept us fed and clothed. Still it was our own place and very comfortable.

John worked part time on the Williams Farm (next to the one we lived on) - at least he didn't have to travel far.

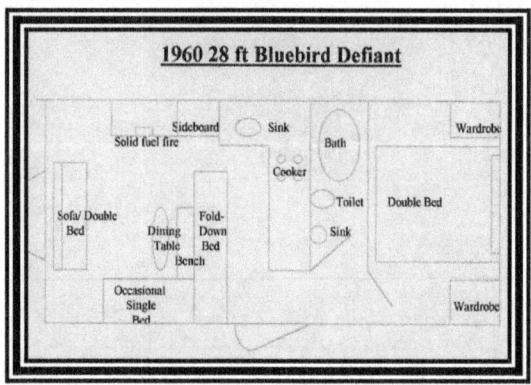

We lived in this at Mill Rigg Farm Stokesley, Brotton Caravan site and Airy Hill Farm Skelton Green between 1960 and 1962

The little 92cc James motorbike gave up the ghost trying to pull us both, mostly uphill, from the Boro so we bought a 250cc BSA, at least it had a proper back seat and not just a cushion on the back mudguard like the James.

After a while we moved to a proper caravan site at Brotton. It had footpaths, hard standings for the van, proper water supplies and drainage. Mother came over with us and started seeing Ted, Johns Uncle.

We still had to travel to the Boro to work on the motorbike. This wasn't too bad in the summer but we had some awful journeys in the bad weather, I lost count of the number of times we came off the thing, but at least we didn't suffer any real injuries. We came off one night in a snowstorm and I had a brown paper package full of dry cleaning which disappeared in the crash. John found it two months later when the snow cleared and the cleaning, particularly my pleated skirt, was still in good order.

When I think back to those journeys, twenty-two miles each way, it was credit to the old motorbikes that we were never late for work, even though at times, busses and cars couldn't get through. One of the firemen told me that John had to be virtually lifted from his bike one very cold morning and practically carried to the hot showers to get him warmed.

We then moved lock stock and barrel to a site at Skelton Green, Henderson's Farm, and shortly after mother married Ted; it was here that while I was doing the family washing in the site washhouse that the poor cat got a dunking. I was using the top loading washing machine when a dog chased the cat in, it shot around the walls onto the draining board, I can see it now back peddling frantically as it slid on into the open top of the oscillating machine. Blowing bubbles and squealing each time it came to the top, I managed to pull the bedraggled thing out and promptly dropped it when it scratched me. It shot off leaving a trail of bubbles never to be seen near the washhouse again.

A New Lease of Life with the RAF

Mother got a Council house at 18 Windermere Drive in Skelton and we joined the RAF and sold the caravans. We were conned by Rowland Caravans when we left the van in their care to sell on our behalf. We had paid £600 for the Bluebird, we sold it at eighteen months old and we expected a sum in the region of £400 to £450. They informed us that they could only get £210 for it. We found out from a friend that worked for them that it had been sold to a family member of the owner; we got the Police to investigate but nothing could be proved so we refused to pay the remaining hire purchase, probably about £200, and let them take us to court, the judge found us guilty of not paying, which was true, but made them pay the Court costs and said that we had to pay the remainder of the HP at the rate of 2s 6p per week, so he was obviously on our side. The bad publicity surrounding the case must have cost them dearly.

18 Newbiggin, Richmond, North Yorkshire

When John had finished his basic training at RAF Bridgnorth he was posted to RAF Catterick for fire training. We moved into a flat in Richmond, number 18 Newbiggin, The house originally formed part of the castle walls and was reputed to be haunted. I am not in the least bit superstitious and I don't believe in ghosts, but there was a definite feeling that someone was in the upstairs rooms whenever I went up there alone. Apparently a young girl had been murdered there in the 16th Century and was said to roam the building. I wouldn't go up there without John; he didn't see or feel anything.

Our Michael, age three at the time, came off his little tricycle on the very steep Bargate Bank and badly cut and bruised his face. Mother visited us four weeks later and his face was still so discoloured that at first she thought he was wearing a mask. He had only just recovered from that when a kid hit him with a lump of wood that put a hole in his head. He seems to get into nearly as much trouble as his dad!

Bridlington East Riding of Yorkshire

When John finished his training he was posted to RAF Carnaby and we moved into a flat, number 4 Marlborough Terrace near the sea front at Bridlington. It was nice there particularly in the winter without the holidaymakers. We went fishing with John one summers day to Flambrough Head, as we were walking along the crowded beach the heavens opened and Michael and I ran with most others to the shelter, John stayed, cast out his line and pulled in four big plaice, the first fish he had caught in weeks. He thought that he had killed them but one of them frightened us to death flapping around in the kitchen later that evening.

The old girl in the ground floor flat set fire to the place one night and a young policeman rescued her, and then alerted the rest of us. She made a complete recovery after we resuscitated her. John was angry because the Fire Brigade didn't have a resuscitator on the fire truck, it was away being serviced. No great damage was done but it could have been a real disaster. Poor Michael, just four at the time, was most upset when he realised that he had left his new fireman uniform behind when we were evacuated.

4 Marborough Terrace, Bridlington. We had the top floor flat.

RAF Driffield, East Riding of Yorkshire

We eventually got a married quarter (33 AMQ) at RAF Driffield and when RAF Carnaby closed down John was posted to RAF Leconfield. We were allowed to stay in the same married quarter. This was the first house that we had lived in on our own and we loved it there. The floors had dark brown lino and they had to be dusted and wax polished continuously to keep them decent. Our Julie was born there without any problems at all; mind she has made up for it since.

Michael and Julie on the steps of No. 33 Airman's Married Quarter, RAF Driffield.

At that time John had a big moustache that he waxed at the ends, I didn't like it at all but he thought it was the bees-knees, that is until sister Shirley and her friend decided to throw a bucket of water over him while he was having a kip in the garden. I didn't know that they were going to do this but I somehow, accidentally of course, just happened to have the camera ready. When the photos were developed his drooping moustache made him look just like the comedian Mr Pastry. And it was shaved off in a flash, I should have thought of that years ago!!

Back Home with Mother

He was next posted to the Far East on an unaccompanied twelve month tour. We moved in with mother at Skelton. The 3-bedroom house was full even before we moved in with Mam, Ted, Shirley, Monica, Tony and Neil and now Mike, Julie and I, if that wasn't bad enough Nanna Goupillot later moved in and caused all kinds of problems. Mam was ill part of the time and I had to keep the house going, keep my job in the Fish and Chip shop and try to write to John every day. This was probably the hardest time of my life and I lost a couple of stone in weight. John hit the roof when he came home because had he realised that we had problems, he could have had us moved into a married quarter. I didn't fancy moving to an RAF Station, where I didn't know anyone. Looking back, maybe I should have done, but at least I knew that it was only for a year.

Julie was only about fifteen months old when John came on leave and she was really upset when she first saw his nearly black face, after the shock wore off she wouldn't leave him alone and would hang onto his leg whenever he moved around.

Doncaster, South Yorkshire

When he eventually came home he was posted to RAF Finningley. We moved into a flat in Kings Rd, Doncaster. It was here that we got Brandy, our mongrel dog. John was working part time painting a house and the owner asked him to drown the little puppy, he was brought home and gave us lots of pleasure for about fourteen years. After a while we moved into a married quarter on the camp. It was here that we met Barry and Adele Staley. Poor Barry was helping an old lady out of the supermarket with her shopping when the shop security pulled him over for shop lifting, the old girl had no intention of paying for the stuff, the staff new this trick and Barry was released having learned another lesson the hard way. We have kept in touch over the years and after a few years we went up to Scotland to visit them, we were admiring Nathan, the new baby thinking he was Simon's or Natasha's, no he was Dell's and Barry's and he is a real charmer.

Michael joined the Cub Scouts and brought a letter home asking parents to attend a meeting, *'We need volunteers to help run the Cubs and Scouts',* we were the only parents there. We had no real choice. We had no experience at all but it was great fun and it was to keep John and I off the streets for over twenty years.

Marham, Norfolk

Our next move was to RAF Marham in Norfolk and we moved straight into a quarter on the station. We were not too happy there because we had problems with our neighbours and John did not like the work. We don't know of anyone that had a good word for that station. Thank goodness John was promoted and moved to Scampton so we only had to put up with it for six months.

We had a Bedford 8 seater van and we would take gangs from the married quarters out to the fields picking fruit and vegetables, I soon learned which lasses could work hard and those that skived and eventually got a good team that worked well. I was able to pay them well because the farmers could rely on us and were prepared to pay more.

We had the van serviced and the next day a wheel fell off, we couldn't prove negligence but we did warn others not to use that garage, fortunately we were going slowly through a village when it happened and no one was hurt, but poor Julie, who was only about three at the time, took it badly and was terrified to go in the van again. We had been working at a village called Holt during the day, that night John was called out to a terrible mid-air collision between a Victor Tanker and a Canberra aircraft that killed all seven airmen just a couple of miles from the farm we were working at.

Scampton, Lincolnshire

RAF Scampton was our next stop and I got a job looking after the kids in the playground, Julie, being Julie, wanted to be at the front of the line of kids, they were having none of this, so she pushed the front lad and they all fell down like a pack of cards and she stood at the front arms folded, nose in the air! I had to pretend I hadn't noticed.

They always seemed to want to run-up the engines of the Vulcan Bombers in the middle of the night and the roar would shake the house. As John would say, "This would be a super aerodrome if it didn't have any aeroplanes!"

I took the Cub Scouts on a trip to Chatsworth House, how that lovely china, porcelain and fancy furniture survived my lot I've no idea, it was touch and go on occasions. John had a party of Scouts cooking the mid-day meal for us in a field and I shall never forget one of the Cubs, Michael Bull, walking down the field, cap on the back of his head glasses askew, socks around his ankles and covered in mud, for all the world like a cross between Just William and Dennis the Menace out of the comics. That wasn't the only problem we had, our car, the Vauxhall Victor decided to snap in half on the rough ground and John had to transfer the lads to other cars, collect the camping kit, and drive back with the back doors held together with string, hoping the police wouldn't spot him. The car finished up on the fire ground being burned on a training exercise.

Return to Germany

RAF Gutersloh in Germany, no problem getting me there, I'm a German, wrong!! I needed a British passport, this caused more trouble than enough. We had to write letters to Germany to prove that I was German, to the British Home Office to prove that I had been an alien. The RAF sorted all the paper work needed for me to get my British Citizenship, they paid most of the costs, all I had to do was pay the small fee needed for the Commissioner of Oaths. It took weeks to sort out before I could get a British passport to travel to my own Country.

I was just over eight when we left Germany and I could only speak English when we returned. It did slowly come back to me when I was amongst Germans again, but my learning of that language was that of a child and I was therefore struggling to try to understand adult vocabulary, I keep promising myself to go to classes to regain a proper understanding of the language. Mind, when we did get sorted it was marvellous to get there and move straight into a flat on the farm at Samptholtz with the Grotehiede family, Charlie, Irmgard and Hendrick, he was just three when we arrived.

Our home at the Grotehiede Farm Germany. We had the top floor.

A dream I had always had of Germany came true that first winter when we saw wild deer playing in the deep snow just in front of the house. The winters in that part of Germany were great, once the snow came it stayed for months and although the temperature was low the snow stayed crisp and with the sun out during the day it was very pleasant. The kids walked on snowshoes and the cars had snow tyres fitted and simply drove on the top of the packed snow.

My dream came true looking out of this window.

Within days Mike, just twelve at the time, was driving in the fields on the big tractor with an eight bladed plough, John was hand milking the cows and Julie and I were helping to feed the animals, horses, pigs, ducks, chickens, cows, and a massive, wild, great dane guard dog, Bruno.

Julie doing the donkey work for Michael and Hendrick.
I didn't like to tell her it was a <u>Dog</u> Cart!

Charlie gave Julie and I seven ducks to rear, they lived in an old van in the field at the back of the house; they started as little balls of fluff and were fully grown in a few months. When they were killed for Christmas our Julie didn't seem to mind pulling their insides out and the feathers off. John was the only one to eat any, we had become too attached to them, we had two and the farmer had two, unfortunately the others were lost to the foxes.

I was babysitting for some neighbours Rudolph and Gundhild. Tara eighteen months old was in bed when I went into the stables to feed the horses, Boris, aged about four, the little darling, locked me in and wouldn't open the door. Tara was screaming, I was pleading, threatening and cursing but he thought this was all great fun. In the end I had to dig my way out under the stable door with an eating fork. His mother and father thought it funny, they didn't believe in chastising the kids, weird! I was most definitely not amused; it cost them a good baby sitter.

John casually waved to his mother in a car going in the opposite direction as we were going to the local shops, he slammed the brakes on when he remembered that he was in Germany and that his mum should be in England. She had been on holiday with friends touring France and Spain, without a word to us, they diverted thousands of miles to pay us a visit. Typical of mother she didn't like Germans because they couldn't speak English and didn't have fish and chips!!

John and I helped to run the Cubs and Scouts on the RAF camp and after a while we were asked to establish Scouting at the Sundern Army Barracks. We had some good times with the lads and eventually I was asked to take on the role of Assistant District Commissioner Leader Training, this meant that I could visit all the other Cub Packs in the District and organise various courses and activities for the leaders and for the boys. John, Michael, Julie, and I have each got tales to tell of our adventures and I suspect that John will get around to writing separate accounts of these at some stage, I do hope so.

The Boys and I on Church Parade Mansergh Barracks, Germany

John was asked to join the volunteer fire brigade in the local village. When he got permission from the RAF he went for his first days training at the Samptholz Fire Station. They rushed him out of the station and into the pub where the training was to begin in earnest. A Westphalia Toast consists of a half litre of beer followed by a schnapps chaser. When they got him home he was apologising in German to our English visitors. Fortunately he was off RAF duties for four days. He was so ill that he needed all of them to recover. He made a vow that he would never drink schnapps again. He swears that he can still taste it in his mouth whenever he thinks about it.

We were shopping in the village when Julie said that she heard a girl speaking English, I investigated and introduced myself to Beryl and Linda Hoste, they lived in the nearby village of Clarholz. Linda and Julie became firm friends, they where both about six at the time. I recall looking out of the window to see Linda and Mike sitting in the pony cart with Julie pulling the thing along. The animals made a lot of noise but you could always hear those two giggling somewhere on the farm, usually at poor Mike's expense.

George Hoste was in the RAF Regiment at Gutersloh, he was one of the smartest men I ever met, I'm sure that he must have gone to bed with a tie on!! We all had to dress up for the parties at one of our houses and these were always posh do's with the best food, wine, china and crystal. George and John would sometimes get blotto and Beryl would have to drive home, it wasn't easy getting George into that little red Renault 4 especially with John trying to pull him out of the other side to get him back into the house for more booze.

George and Beryl had arranged to take Michael with them on a camping tour of Europe. George had planned the whole trip with military precision, even down to the roster for the chores. Unfortunately Michael's passport didn't arrive in time so they had to go without him, we were all very upset about that, and poor George had to re-write the rosters.

Sadly Beryl and George have passed away, we have lost two of our best friends. We are pleased that Linda keeps in touch with us. She treats us like aunt and uncle and we hope that she always will.

An outing in the new Renault 16 with The Hoste family George, Beryl, and Linda

With the help of the German Fire Service I was able to contact my Dad, we had lost touch with him and it was good to see him after twenty-four years. We travelled through East Germany to West Berlin to see him and his new wife Inge and they came to the farm to visit us. He died in 1977 but at least we had been together again after so long.

Lachmanstrasse with my Dad 1972

Percy Pritchard helped us with the Scouts and Cubs and would load his plastic tripod (Robin Reliant) to the gunwales with camping kit and fly around at breakneck speed, our Mike loved riding in that thing with him, how he didn't roll it was anyone's guess. He was a good sport and would help anyone.

The firemen serviced their cars in the fire station at Gutersloh and Percy drove his car over the pit just as they all did, but he had forgotten that his was a three wheeler and it took all the firemen on duty, and all in stitches, to lift it back out again, poor Percy will never live that one down.

We visited Antwerp for the day with the Scouts and we were on a cruise boat on the river when the wave from a passing oil tanker caused the mooring lines of an American Destroyer and a Submarine to break. As the submarine set off sideways down the river the crew popped out of every hatch then shot down again and came up, this time with their lifejackets on. They just managed to get engine power on in time to prevent it hitting the quayside. By the time we got close to the Destroyer the crew were hauling the ship back to the berth using a long line. As you can imagine our Scouts were calling the rhythm to the sailors and having a good laugh at their expense.

I don't know whether the Americans realised that we were the same group when we visited them the next day, but they made us very welcome. I can see Julie, hands on hips again, telling the Captain and First Officer how to run the ship. We all swapped caps with the sailors and had to spend the rest of the camp wearing white floppy sailors hats. One of them got a Brownie hat from Julie and another got my expensive Leaders hat.

You can read about the problems getting to see my dad in Berlin in John's life story *The Boro Boy*. Suffice here to say that it was great to see him again after so many years and that he was able to see his Grandchildren before he past away in the late 70's.

Because my Grandmother and Aunty Heidi were over sixty we were able to get them out of East Germany for a short holiday. My Mum was staying with us in our house at Topferstrasse in Gutersloh. We didn't tell her that her Mum was coming for a visit and when the doorbell rang we sent Mum to answer it, they didn't recognise each other at first after twenty-four years but when it dawned on them the tears flowed and the screams of joy could be heard for miles, we had also arranged to have Aunt Gretchen, Uncle Ernst, Cousin Heinz, Uncle Ted and Neil with us at the same time. One night, after a party, we had Reg Matthews, Pete McAllister, Andy Whitehead and Percy Pritchard staying as well, poor Reg had to cook breakfast for fifteen!!

The big reunion, Aunties Gretel, Heidi, My Grandma, Uncles Ted and Ernst

This was one of the nicest things that we have ever been able to organise. This meeting eventually became even more important because Grandma was to die before the Berlin Wall came down and freedom to travel was possible again.

It took a long time but Mum did get through the Berlin Wall.

Northern Ireland

After Germany it was normal to be posted back to the UK, however we had not expected to finish up at RAF Bishops Court in Northern Ireland, and in 1973 it was not a good time to be there. However we moved into a house in the fishing village of Ardglass in County Down and we could not have been made more welcome anywhere.

John, he was already there, had told us not to talk to anyone on the journey over on the Heysham-Belfast ferry. Julie, being Julie, got chatting to one of the ship's crew, he must have realised that I was concerned so he came over to reassure me, I could have died when he said that he knew that we would be on his ship and that we were going to live in the village of Ardglass, he even knew that we would be living in Kildare street, it turned-out that he was a relative of the landlord of our house. We soon learned that everyone in Ireland knows what everyone else is doing!!

We have all heard tales of the way of life in Ireland and we found that it is not all myth. Barbara Hibberd and I would travel around on the local bus, we couldn't believe our eyes the first time when we found that the bus delivered petrol, milk, groceries, sheep, live chickens and would stop at the door of the houses to let people off. The driver would have a pad with messages for different people on the route. He know them all by first names and remembered ours after the first trip, Babs and Vee. On the days we used the bus he would stop right outside of our door to pick us up, then drop us at the door when we returned.

Riding in the car with rubber duck (one of Mikes teachers) was a nightmare. She had never had a driving test (they were not introduced there until the 60's) and being a driver before that meant that she was exempt. She picked up Barbara and I to go to the Women's Institute each week and almost reversed us all into the harbour one night. She never seemed to know which side of the road to drive on, so it was always a bear knuckle ride for Babs and I.

The view from 6 Kildare Street Ardglass, County Down, Northern Ireland.
1973

We created a section of the St John Ambulance Brigade on the Station mainly for the Cadets, we were affiliated to a group in the nearby town of

Downpatrick. We won most of the First Aid competitions that we entered into and had lots of trophies to prove it.

We acquired an ex Military Ambulance which our Michael spent hours renovating and painting to get it ready for duties throughout the Province. We attended all sorts of functions from Horse Trials to Motor Racing but most of our casualties came from the football and rugby teams on camp. Michael and John would often be asked to look after people in the hospital casualty waiting room because there was such a shortage of hospital staff. Michael loved getting involved even though he was only fifteen at the time. I suppose it was a good grounding for the work that he does so well now.

The Goup's in the St John Ambulance Brigade in Northern Ireland

We heard that help was needed to help with a handicapped child, Mary Thompson, she was a little darling, she was brain damaged and needed to be given exercises for six hours each day, this was to much for the parents George and Lilly, so people volunteered to do one hourly sessions at different times, we were able to do a couple of sessions most days. We became close friends with them and still send Christmas greetings, sadly Lilly died in the early 90's leaving poor George with Mary and the younger daughter Alexis.

I started a Cub Scout Pack in the local Church Hall and we had some great times. We organised a day outing to the Tyrela Beach for all the Packs in the County and the compulsory dress was to be in the Western style, we all dressed as Cowboys and Indians and had a competition for the best Chuck Wagon. We then had to race them down the beach and over the sand dunes, this wrecked most of the wagons, then we finished with a barbecue and camp fire sing-along. It was one of many great days.

In the pits before the big race.
Wagon masters Carol Evans and I give last minute instructions.

We got a call from the guardroom at midnight, while camping with the Youth Club kids on the airfield, to say that our Tony (my brother) was at the ferry terminal at Larne and would we go and collect him. We had no idea that he was coming over. John found him sound asleep in the doorway of the terminal building, not a care in the world. He wasn't quite so relaxed after they had driven back through one of the worst nights of violence in the history of Belfast. Mind he slept it off for most of the two weeks that he stayed with us.

We tended not to worry too much about the troubles but it did affect us on occasions. I was in bed one night when I heard a bang, I said to John that a bomb had gone off, John was sure that it was a car back-firing but when he went to investigate, a shop and a garage had been blown up in the next street to ours. The Naafi on camp was blown apart by a milk-churn bomb and we had some bomb scares most of which proved to be hoaxes.

We were on a Wives Club shopping trip in the RAF coach to Bangor, just as we were going back to the coach there was an almighty bang and the Woolworth shop was destroyed, thankfully no one was hurt, but we had all been in there at some time during that day.

Some of the Ladies of the Bishops Court Wives Club

I was angry with the bus driver one day when I found out that he had put Mike off the bus because he had been larking about, (our Mike larking about, never!!), not the sort of place for a young English lad to be walking on his own in the countryside.

The RAF coach was ambushed in Newcastle (Northern Ireland) whilst picking up servicemen for work and I was annoyed that the holes had not been repaired and the blood not cleaned up before it was used for the kids two days later, the kids thought it was great. After I complained the RAF covered the holes with black masking tape, I suppose it makes a change from the usual miles of red tape!

Ready for another trip - bullet holes and all!!

Back to Catterick

After three years in Ireland John was posted to RAF Catterick on instructional duties and we moved into a married quarter in Yarde Ave on the camp. It was a nice three- bedroomed detached house but after only a few months we had to move out and into the Chapel Riggs complex on Leeming Lane. We continued our Scouting and St. John Ambulance Brigade activities. I helped to run the Cub Pack in the village and I accepted the post of Nursing Officer with the St. John. One of the highlights was being introduced to HRH The Princess Margaret when she visited our Ambulance Cadet Division, she was charming and very much at ease with the children and she seemed to take great care to speak to them all.

Having a laugh with HRH The Princess Margaret

We met her again when John and I were invited to St. James Palace for cocktails, something to do with the RAF Benevolent Fund. It was a breath-taking experience to be in such wonderful surroundings and with so many important people, HRH, Douglas Bader, some MP's and Lords including Lord Macmillan and many others. As we walked up the massive staircase towards the armoury John said, "I can't believe that this is happening to us". As we entered the Queen Elizabeth Room the usher frightened us to death when he shouted, "Sergeant and Mrs. Goupillot," then introduced us to the various dignitaries. It all sounds very pompous and officious but they all made us feel comfortable at once.

We asked the photographer if he would take a picture of us near the throne, he said that he was very sorry but that he could only take official shots, then he said profoundly,"You know that you have been here, you know what it all looks like and what it feels like, so why do you need photographs?" He was right of course.

The invitation to St. James Palace

We used to run the disco for the kids on camp and from the village. One evening we had a Cowboy theme and fancy dress was compulsory. John's brother Geoff arranged for the charity group of adult cowboys from the roughest pub in Middlesborough, The Albion, to attend. We hadn't told the kids what was going to happen, but half-way through the evening the Cowboys and Cowgirls arrived in full kit, the goodies walked to one end of the dance-floor and the baddies to the other, you could have heard a pin drop, John walked into the middle to introduce them and before he could say a word they all opened up on him with blank shot, well, the noise inside the hall was deafening, it frightened some of the kids, and John, but they soon got over the shock and were joining in the fun with sharp shooting and fast draw competitions. They may have been a rough bunch but they gave those children a night to remember and must have spent a small fortune on ammunition letting the youngsters fire those very realistic guns all evening. We could still smell the gun-smoke when we returned a week later.

At the discos the kids had to get up and dance - the punishment for offenders was having to dance with John, or me it worked. I'm sure the kids will always remember those discos when they hear the Hoky Coky because that was the signal for their final dance of the night. Discipline was always tight and we had very little trouble, when we did have any they knew that their dads would be informed as a matter of course. Mind it wasn't all roses with the kids; John talked Garry Steel down from the Church roof after he threatened to jump. Just a few weeks later he broke into and wrecked the inside of our caravan. I couldn't face going into it again so we bought a new one.

When ever kids were hurt it was always our fault for not looking after them properly. How you could stop a youngster running into a branch of a tree in the woods or prevent a child getting impaled on a metal bar while playing I just don't know. It was times like this when we felt like giving it up, however we were more interested in giving the kids a good time than listening to the few ungrateful parents, some of whom couldn't give a damn what happened to the kids until something went wrong.

John was promoted to Sergeant and later to Flight Sergeant; this meant that John had to get involved with the social life of the Sergeants Mess. Ladies nights were posh do's - the men dressed in Mess Kit, dickey bows, cumber bands and medals polished. We - the girls, had to dress up in evening dress and we were spoiled all evening with the best food, expensive wines and chamber music and grand speeches from guest speakers then dancing through the night to some great dance bands. All a bit heady but fantastic some memories.

A good do in the Sergeants Mess with Kath and Brian Roberts

It was here that we first met Marjorie Stokell, she came dashing over for Johns help when her friend Kate Hunter collapsed. Sadly John was unable to revive her and Marjorie came to rely on me and John for support and help with funeral arrangements etc. Shortly after that her Mam died suddenly and then her Sister Mary; we helped again with the funerals. Not long after Alex Hunter took ill and we took Marjorie to hospital each day, he too died after a short illness leaving Marjorie with no friends or family nearby. Alex left his bungalow, Scotia, 37 Leeming Lane to Marjorie in his Will. She sold her old house 40 Leeming Lane and move into Scotia, 37 Leeming Lane.

We have never spent so much money in such a sort time as we did when we helped her to buy a new car, central heating, new kitchen, dining suit, bedroom suit, gas fire, carpets and lots of new clothes, £19,000 in less than a week. We told her to spend it on herself, as folk would only fight over it if she died and left it in the bank, how true that statement proved in the end, at least she lived the rest of her life in a comfortable home. She spent a lot of time with us and we had many happy holidays at home and abroad. We had some good times up in Scotland with her friends Jack and Janet Hall. We often stayed fishing at the cottage at Skerrey on the North coast. John fished all week once and caught nothing. When we visited the local pub John was told by the local poacher to leave the boot of the car open, when we returned to the cottage John found a massive salmon in the boot. Jack set to work gutting, slicing and cooking the thing, it was delicious, it was the first time we had eaten fresh salmon.

We laughed when Marjorie bought a heather plant at the local shop without realising that the cottage we were living in was surrounded by the same plants.

Happy days with Marjorie, Jack and Janet at Skerrey, Scotland

We were warned that Jack didn't like the English very much but he seemed to take to us all right and spent hours talking to John about flyfishing and woodworking. When he found out that John had served in the Scots Greys he wanted to see if John had learned anything about being a Scot, so off we went to the pub. John had been in hospital whilst in the Army with whisky poisoning and had not drunk any whisky since he was eighteen, however Jack was very persuasive and they each drank eight or ten double whiskies, each as stubborn as the other, they wouldn't give in, John showed no ill effects until lunch time the next day. We had set off in the caravan and stopped at the Caithness factory at Perth, John was a long time in the toilet so I ask a chap to investigate, sure enough he was so ill he couldn't leave the loo, he was ill for a further three days, Jack thought this was great, John didn't!! Credit to Jack, he never pushed him to drink again after that. Jack and Janet died soon after each other in the early 90's - it was a sad loss to us all. John always said that if he had to choose one man to represent the Scots it would be Jack.

We both stopped smoking just before we left Ireland, and without telling John, I saved the money that we would have spent on cigarettes. After a year we were able to pay cash for our first touring caravan, a four birth Sprite Musketeer.

Money saved from stopping smoking bought this out first touring caravan

Scampton then Demob

Right out of the blue someone at RAF Records decided that John needed a posting to an operational unit, when he was promoted to Flight Sargent he was asked if he would stay on at Catterick. He enjoyed the work at the Fire School so he was pleased to accept and expected to stay there for a few more years. Why Scampton is anyone's guess, it was a busy station when we were last there but now it was probably the quietest station in the UK, the Vulcan's had all gone and most of the staff, all that remained were the Red Arrows Display Team and they seemed to spend most of the time away. All John had to look after were twenty fireman and three fire trucks; he was bored to tears. He tried to exchange postings after eight months with other Flight Sergeants at Catterick that wanted Scampton but Records said no he needed operational experience, he had twenty-five years experience by this time, how much more did they think he needed, so when the chance came to move to a civilian teaching post with the Civil Aviation Authority, he was off.

I had my problems with the Red Arrows, they would sometimes practice over the airfield and the dye from the coloured smoke would play havoc with my washing. John requested that notice be given when smoke was to be used, this was accepted, that then gave us housewives the chance to organise washing on other days, it was a very rare occurrence for the Military to take married family problems into consideration for such things!

They practiced most days but we never got sick of watching them.

Although we carried on Scouting with the small numbers of kids and we had some friends it was not the same as the busy units that we had been used too. Although I was apprehensive about leaving the RAF after so many years, I was not sorry to leave Scampton this time around.

The Oaklands

1983 a year to remember. It was our 25th wedding anniversary. Mike and Julie were married, we came out of the RAF, John was starting a new career with the CAA and we bought our first house, 28 the Oaklands, Middleton-One-Row, Near Darlington. We had problems moving into the new house, John and I were getting rid of the married quarter at Scampton and we asked Marjorie if she would look after the furniture as it was moved into the Oaklands, the only problem was that the previous tenants, the Geldarts, had not moved out and when she and the furniture van arrived they were merrily having breakfast still with their furniture filling the house. They were eventually asked to move out into the garden to await their removers. It took us a further two months and threats of, "I'll burn the bleep bleep lot if you don't come and take it away," to eventually get the garage and greenhouse cleared of their property.

We had good neighbours including Bob and Val De'Ath and we enjoyed living there. We had some furniture made to suit the house including a dining room suite, a three piece suite for the lounge and lamp shades etc.

John seemed to be enjoying his job at the Civil Aviation Authority Fire Service Training School at Teesside Airport and I got a job at Kings Hardware store in Darlington. I have fond memories of the place and the people the Christmas parties were always a big hit. I have lasting friendships and still keep in touch with some of them.

While John was away in Africa our Monica arranged for a Tarzan Kiss-a-Gram to come to the shop, all very embarrassing but a great laugh. The boss Len Barker would have a party at the drop of a hat, he was a good manager and always had time for his staff. We all got really good Christmas presents, usually good quality items from the shop.
One problem that we did have was that the Baby Shop was next door which meant that I was always in and out buying bits for the grandchildren.

The gang at King & Co Darlington Christmas party Len doing his stuff as Santa

Our Mike was sent from The Queen's Flight at the end of his tour to the Fire School at Catterick and they moved into a house at the Shearwater Estate in Darlington and it was here that Rachel was born.

Michael at the open day at The Queen's Flight

Julie lived in our caravan on a site near Richmond for a while then moved to RAF Odiham in Hampshire, our Darren was born at the Military Hospital in Aldershot. They eventually moved back to Catterick and bought a house in Darlington. It was nice to have them all near us for a while.

The 1978 Ace Award 14/4 (tourer)
Both Julie and Mike lived in this whilst waiting for RAF Married Quarters.
Julie and Andy had their honeymoon in it in the Lake District.

Andy came out of the RAF and joined the Leeds Bradford Airport as a fireman and after his basic training they move to Thorpe Willoughby. I was on an outing with the company to Blackpool when our Darren was born. John was collecting our new car, the SAAB, and the clock on the car was registered as being set at the precise moment that he was born. Bob and Val took us to the annual dinner dances at the Free Masons Lodge at Bishop Auckland, these were really nice do's and the food was great, the dancing was normally old time so John couldn't try his favourite Charlston too much, he had to dance properly for a change.

We would have liked to have continued with Scouting and St John's but our services were not needed here as they had been in the military environment so we both retired after over twenty-five years service that we really enjoyed.

I was called from work because John had been hurt, I was disgusted when I arrived at the hospital to find him still in casualty laying on a stretcher in the dirty water that was dripping from his fire kit, he had been there for an hour and nobody had seen to him, I raised the roof and got things moving, thank goodness he wasn't badly hurt and was back at work in a few weeks.

John was promoted to Divisional Officer, with the CAA Aerodrome Inspectorate near Gatwick Airport, so we were on the move again, I was expecting to stay in Darlington until we retired, never mind at least we are experienced movers!!

1983-89
28 The Oaklands, Middleton-One-Row Darlington.
The first house of our own.

Camelot Close

More problems moving! We were delayed by three days coming back from our holiday in Hawaii, this meant that Marjorie and I had to travel straight up to Darlington from the airport, to pack and move the furniture and John had to stay at Southwater in Horsham, West Sussex to sort out the house and check that the carpets were down ready to move in. Needless to say they were not layed and as always the company had a million excuses for the delay.
Anyway we eventually got moved in and sorted out. It was a nice looking house with four bedrooms but was not well built, the walls were like cardboard and the floors creaked from day one.

1989-97
58 Camelot Close, Southwater, Horsham, West Sussex
Through no fault of our own this property became a financial disaster.

The Aussies, Barry, Jane, Mark and Rebecca came to England for a year to find the best treatment for Beckie and we became firm friends. I can hear Beckie roaring with laughter when I went head first over the top of the sledge and into a ditch on the cricket field; she wanted me to do it again!! We used to go over to them most Saturday nights to play Trivial Pursuit and a natter, it was nice for us to get out. We were all sad when they had to go back, I've heard recently that Mark has come back to the UK to play cricket for some club in the South.

Jane, Rebecca, Barry, Mark Wadsworth (the Aussies)
John never did tell me how silly I looked in that Russian hat.

John was now the chief inspector of most of the aerodromes in the UK and this meant working very long hours and he spent most of his time on the road. I got a job with the Sun Alliance Insurance Company in Horsham so this meant that I didn't get too bored. Once again I have fond memories and I made many friends.

It was nice being in the South near the coast, we could drive to Worthing or Brighton in a few minutes or go hunting around the antique shops in Arundel or the big antique fairs at Goodwood Race Course, I got most of my Hummel collection from there. John bought me the little girl with the umbrella from a shop in Yarm for a birthday present, I particularly like that one because it reminds me of my childhood in Germany, I seem to remember a picture that looked very similar to it, I think it was probably at my grandma's house.

I was working on my 50th birthday and the staff made a big fuss with cards and flowers etc. Late in the afternoon I heard a commotion, when I looked up there was John dressed as Fireman Sam with a sign round his neck with the words "Kiss a Gran, Happy Birthday Vera," He didn't think I would recognise him in all that kit but I would know him anywhere. He had arranged with Sun Alliance and the Fire Brigade to come up a ladder and through my office window but the Hydraulic Platform was out of action on that day, never mind it was still a lovely surprise.

John as Fireman Sam with a Kiss-a-Gran

The trips to the Scilly Isles were great fun, the details of these are written in John's book *The Boro Boy*.

Sadly Poor Marjorie hurt her leg getting off the coach at Victoria Bus Station in London where we were waiting to pick her up to come with us on one of these trips and I am sure that was the start of the series of problems that resulted in her death a couple of years later.

This flight over Land's End was to be my first in a light aircraft

Cricketers Green

We had problems selling the house in Southwater because the housing market was in a slump so when the opportunity arose we had to get rid of it while we had a buyer. We lost £84,000 on the deal and this meant that we had to buy Cricketers Green with a mortgage. We had hoped to sell the house in the south for a profit and pay cash for our retirement home. I had always thought that we were fairly lucky in most things, but now, when it mattered most, it let us down.

We moved to the Leeds area to be near Julie who was not well and could have needed our help. Had that not been the case we would probably have moved to the Stokesley/Great Ayton area were I had lived before we were married.

The move itself was no picnic, we hired a large truck and found that it wasn't big enough, so at the last minute we had to get another. Loaded to busting point we set off from West Sussex as it was getting dark with John driving the front truck, Mike in the large one and me driving the car in the middle. We got as far as the M25 and it started snowing and the further North we got the worse it became, we could hardly see in some areas, poor Mike had trouble with his windscreen wipers and had to struggle on until we stopped for fuel. Once we fixed that we had to continue because one van had to be back in Horsham the next day, the other could be returned to the Leeds depot. This was the first time I had ever driven any distance in the dark. That's us, if there is an easy way to do anything we'll chose the hard way!!

I didn't like Cricketers Green very much when we first moved in but we have improved it dramatically and I am now fond of the place. We have good neighbours and it is nice to be near at least one set of grandchildren, and really it's only a couple of hours from our Mike's but it would be nice if we could have all be together in the same area, then we could spend more time with the grandchildren.

2 Cricketers Green, Rawdon, Leeds, West Yorkshire

Unfortunately John still had a year to go before retirement after we sold the house so he lived in the caravan, he always said that he preferred that to living in digs because he was not answerable to anyone else, but I think now that I should have insisted that he moved into better accommodation. He had problems at work with the new managers, all of whom had no fire or airport experience, and he had to travel up and down to Gatwick each week. All of these things started to get him down until in the end he walked away from the job before it gave him a breakdown, as had happened to all four of his fellow inspectors. Sadly he was too late and when he went for stress counselling he was already in a bad way. It has taken three years to recover but even now he gets the odd bad days.

I was glad to get out of the way at times and working part time at the airport for Alpha Flight Services was a nice break. I have now retired and at times we are under each others feet. I think that I was under a lot of pressure during that time as well, I found it difficult to talk to him at times and I was always afraid in case I said the wrong thing, trying to keep the balance often made me feel very stressed and I am sure it didn't help me having high blood pressure on top of that. To top it all John was the executor for Marjorie's Will along with her Solicitor, her relatives in Australia gave them both a hard time accusing them of all kinds of skulduggery, this put even more strain on John when he was just starting to recover.

Since John started to get better and I have started going to the gym and walking regularly I now feel much better in myself and I can cope better with John's occasional relapses.
John had a workshop built in the garden and Tony the builder asked him if he would like to do the labouring, well I think that that was the real start of John's recovery, it gave him something positive to do and took his mind of other things. He worked with

Tony for a couple of years and he reckons he was the oldest apprentice builder in the business!!
He has also been working with the CAA International Services in various parts of the World he loves the work and he has been able to regain his confidence.

We have recently joined the Wharfedale German Circle and it is interesting to get involved with people with connections in Germany. There are only two of us actually Germans and we speak and understand less of the language than most of the others. We have booked ourselves onto a German language course starting in November, that might help a bit. We are thinking of going to Germany again for our main holiday next year so it would help to understand more of the language and the culture. My problem is that I left Germany when I was under nine years old and I therefore only learned the language of a child, and, as I have said earlier, when I first came to England I wanted to forget German as quickly as I could.

We went to Oklahoma in the USA to visit Hector and Linda and went over to Texas to call on Jackie and Jason. John plans to write about our holidays in a separate account and I am sure that the trip to the States was at least as exiting as the other holidays that we have had.

One of the hardest things we had to face was Michael and Lynne splitting up, it came right out of the blue, however, Mike has since married Sue and is very happy and we have gained two more grandchildren Natalie and Greg. Rachel lives nearby and spends a lot of time with Mike unfortunately David has broken contact with his Dad but we are all hoping he will come around in time.

I was made redundant from Alpha Services in 2003 and I am beginning to settle down, we go for walks most days and have made friends with Richard and Eve. We go out most Wednesdays to Skipton for shopping and lunch and odd trips to Whitby for the skate at Trenchers Fish and Chip shop.

Poor John has a whole new millennium to start writing about! Never mind it keeps him in mischief!!

Printed in Great Britain
by Amazon

45892782R00046